Real People

Jackie Robinson

By Philip Abraham

Children's Press®
A Division of Scholastic Inc.
New York / Toronto / London / Auckland / Sydney
Mexico City / New Delhi / Hong Kong
Danbury, Connecticut

Photo Credits: Cover, pp. 11, 13, 15 © Hulton/Archive; pp. 5, 17 © Hulton/Archive/Sporting News; p. 7 © Genevieve Naylor/Corbis; pp. 9, 21 © Bettmann/Corbis; p. 19 © Hulton/Archive/New York Times Co./Meyer Liebowitz
Contributing Editor: Jennifer Silate
Book Design: Christopher Logan

Visit Children's Press on the Internet at:
http://publishing.grolier.com

Library of Congress Cataloging-in-Publication Data

Abraham, Philip, 1970–
Jackie Robinson / by Philip Abraham.
    p. cm. — (Real people)
  Includes bibliographical references and index.
Summary: Introduces Jackie Robinson, the first African American to play major league baseball.
  ISBN 0-516-23950-3 (lib. bdg.) — ISBN 0-516-23605-9 (pbk.)
  1. Robinson, Jackie, 1919–1972—Juvenile literature. 2. Baseball players—United States—Biography—Juvenile literature. [1. Robinson, Jackie, 1919–1972. 2. Baseball players. 3. African Americans—Biography.] I. Title II. Real people (Children's Press)

  GV865.R6 A47 2002
  796.357′092—dc21
  [B]   2001032339

Contents

Meet Jackie Robinson.

5

Jackie was married to a woman named Rachel.

They had three children.

Jackie loved **sports**.

He played football.

Jackie also played baseball.

Jackie was the first **African-American** to play **major league baseball**.

Jackie played for the Brooklyn Dodgers.

He had many **fans**.

15

Jackie won many **awards**.

He was a great baseball player.

Jackie also wanted
to help people.

When he stopped playing
baseball, he helped others.

Jackie Robinson was a great man.

21

New Words

African-American (**af**-ruh-kuhn uh-**mehr**-uh-kuhn) Americans of African family origin

awards (uh-**wordz**) prizes given to the winners of a contest

fans (**fanz**) people who are very interested in someone or something

major league baseball (**may**-juhr **leeg bays**-bahl) the highest level of professional baseball in the United States

sports (**sports**) games or contests that require physical skills

To Find Out More

Books

A Picture Book of Jackie Robinson
by David A. Adler
Holiday House

Jackie Robinson
by Kenneth Rudeen
HarperCollins Children's Books

Web Site

Afro-Americ@: Jackie Robinson
http://www.afroam.org/history/Robinson/intro.html
Learn about Jackie Robinson's life and career on this Web site.

Index

About the Author

Philip Abraham is a freelance writer. He works in New York City.

Reading Consultants

Kris Flynn, Coordinator, Small School District Literacy, The San Diego County Office of Education

Shelly Forys, Certified Reading Recovery Specialist, W.J. Zahnow Elementary School, Waterloo, IL

Sue McAdams, Former President of the North Texas Reading Council of the IRA, and Early Literary Consultant, Dallas, TX

24